# MATCH.COMical

## Three sisters attempt online dating in search of ONE good date.

by

## Candace, Bonnie, and Ellen

### Written with Tammy Mathews

Bloomington, IN  Milton Keynes, UK

authorHOUSE

AuthorHouse™
1663 Liberty Drive, Suite 200
Bloomington, IN 47403
www.authorhouse.com
Phone: 1-800-839-8640

AuthorHouse™ UK Ltd.
500 Avebury Boulevard
Central Milton Keynes, MK9 2BE
www.authorhouse.co.uk
Phone: 08001974150

First published by AuthorHouse 7/25/2006

ISBN: 1-4259-2900-1 (e)
ISBN: 1-4259-2905-2 (sc)

Library of Congress Control Number: 2006903096

Printed in the United States of America
Bloomington, Indiana

This book is printed on acid-free paper.

Photo of Candace: © Annie Dobb/www.hobofoto.net
Photo of Bonnie: Steven Shofner

# FOREWORD

All of us have such high hopes of meeting the man of our dreams. We have tried the traditional meeting places: bars, grocery stores, church, singles mixers, the library, hardware stores, Chippendales, etc. While we have had successes, the failures are too numerous to mention. Before losing hope, we are ready to try the latest craze...Internet dating.

Each of us prepared a personality profile which will tell our potential dates a little bit about each of us. They can then decide if we would make a good match and send along an email introduction. This is where things get SCARY.

You are now about to meet our "matches" through their own words. Names have been changed to protect the guilty. Prepare yourself, reader, you may laugh, you may cry, you may swear off dating forever. One thing is for sure, though, you will have the time of your life.

You are now about to enter the lion's den, so keep your feet and hands inside the armchair!

# CONTENTS

# Allow Me To Introduce Myself...
# I'm Mr. Perfect

We wanted to start with our favorite group of "matches." We have all met these guys at some point in our lives. They are absolutely perfect and only wish that they could meet a woman who was half the man they are.

"I want to meet an attractive ADULT who uses her head for more than a place to display her vast assortment of make-up. I am from the South and consider myself a Southern Gentleman, so I hesitate to mention this quality that I consider very important in a relationship. From my father's lips... "Wild in the bedroom, but a lady in public." I will not lie and will not tolerate a liar. My sense of humor is a bit warped which leads many people to believe I am a pervert...not so."

**"Southern Gentleman?" The lack of respect for women leads me to believe he means Southern Afghanistan Gentleman.**

"Hi. I am new to the system so I apologize for not having a photograph. Let me partially remedy that by drawing an inadequate word picture. I am 6'1", 185 lbs, brown hair and eyes. I am a kind and gentle lawyer (yes, there are such animals) who has at various times been accused of being very bright, a terrific listener, a good conversationalist, and good company. Oh yes, I can also get some affidavits to the effect that I am cute. Some of the signers have now left their institutionalized living quarters."

**The affidavits were signed Lorena Bobbitt and Phyllis Diller.**

"To control SPAM, I now allow incoming messages only from senders I have approved beforehand. If you would like to be added to my list of approved senders, please fill out the short request form below. If I approve you, your original message will be forwarded to my inbox."

**Does the phrase "control freak" ring a bell? Why does anyone need to control canned ham?**

"Ok, I'm working on quitting smoking! I'm just looking to find someone I find attractive to hang out with, go out to dinner and travel with. I'm taking some time for myself right now (I've earned it) and I like to live life very well. Do you like Maui? I just have an urge...at the very least I promise you that. I will be totally honest with you and won't play games with you. I'm open, caring and generous and I've been told I have a nice butt. Can we talk?"

**Maui and a nice butt...what else is there?**

"I've learned that the majority of women on this site don't watch TV, in fact, some don't even own one. They're far too busy filling each of their rare free moments with hiking, SCUBA and sky diving, and riding their horses and Harleys. I've learned that the majority of women are in their element only near a beach and must, therefore, be enduring a miserable existence here in the desert. I've learned that even though men are 90% visual while women care more about what's inside an individual, I shouldn't expect a response unless I have a picture posted. I've learned that most women here don't need a man in their lives, they don't even necessarily want one, but now that the important matters of child rearing and their careers have been addressed, they may be open to such a possibility (hallelujah chorus please). I've learned that by simply having a gym membership you automatically qualify for a body type of 'athletic and toned.' I've learned that the majority of women on here 'love to laugh.' What a refreshing change from those who find it miserable to be happy. I've learned that requesting that a man earn in excess of $150,000/year is actually a measure of the ambition and focus, the money isn't really important. I've learned that a large number of the women here are confused and have no idea why they are doing online dating. If you are physically and emotionally available enough to be able to plan your activities; if you're emotionally divorced from your last relationship; if you appreciate the value of a good spellchecker; if you know the difference between 'everyday' and 'every day', 'workout' and 'work out', I'd love to hear from you."

**Perhaps this lovely specimen would be better off with a blow-up doll. Then she *might* irritate him less.**

"I keep my profile hidden because I'm well-known in business circles and these sites are like an advertisement for yourself. I will leave my profile open for the next 24 hours, so you may read it. I have the time and financial ability to devote to that special someone. I only work enough hours to keep my life fulfilled. I'm not some guy looking for an occasional good time. I think two people need to become friends first, and see where that relationship takes them. I'm a decent, honest, sincere guy looking for those same qualities in someone to share my life with."

**Sounds like there is some potential here. He shouldn't be embarrassed, however, to be seen online by someone who may know him. Be proud of everything you do.**

"Hi there. I swore I wouldn't do this again, but then I saw you and got sucked in again. You sound like you are exactly what I have been waiting for. The fantasy alone is worth the $29.99 for a month. I haven't even filled out my profile as I don't intend to deal with the 200 lb. women that call themselves 'average build' (maybe for an SUV that is average). I think I look pretty good and much younger than my 59 years."

**He has got a way with words doesn't he? He is a real charmer.**

"Independent, successful, professional guy. I'm told that I am classy, interesting, intriguing, a gentleman, witty, successful, attractive (younger and better than the photo) and kind. As a former football and basketball player, I have kept in shape and always will. I am well educated (three degrees) and well traveled (about 48 countries)."

**Sound too good to be true? It was. Both Candace and Bonnie went on a date with him. Both times, he was more impressed with himself than any woman ever would or could be.**

"I am a 58-year old guy in a 6'0", 180lbs, 40's body who has a zest for living a healthy, active life. I must confess to an accent residual from my Australian birth where I lived until I obtained by PhD in theoretical chemistry. My passion, after you should this key fit into your lock, is sailing my 43' sloop. I am partial to romantic movies. I loved *You've Got Mail* and *Notting Hill*. Who knows where this might lead?"

**Who is he trying to fool? He has a PhD in theoretical chemistry and his favorite movies are *You've Got Mail* and *Notting Hill*? He might be *too* in touch with his feminine side.**

I am six feet two inches tall. Two hundred pounds of blue twisted steel. My eyes are blue, hair is brown and it is all on my head. I am sixty-five years old. I realize your age limit is sixty, so you may have a real problem about age. However, I promise you will not be disappointed. I look my age, but I am healthy and work out. No pork belly here! I know how to relate to a woman, I am not your standard egocentric male piggy. I am able to take care of someone, spoil her to rottenness. What I am saying, without being embarrassed because I don't want you to think I am offering to buy you, is that I have an ample income, more than ample. I am in the process of buying another airplane. I hope this will pique your curiosity enough to get you to respond."

**But enough about him...what do you think of him?**

"I was looking through all these ads on this site thinking to myself, look at all of these poor, desperate, lonely women...and then I saw your ad and thought to myself, hey here's someone that I should email. So I thought I'd write and see if you're as interesting on the inside as you are in the picture. I am a manager and for obvious reasons do not date clients or co-workers. That limits my opportunities to meet women. That's why I am trying internet dating. I could stand on my front porch waiting for my fairy godmother to deliver Cinderella to me, but I would get blisters long before that happened."

**Why isn't this hillbilly wearing shoes on his front porch? Maybe the "poor, desperate, lonely women" should let him know that it was Cinderella that lost her shoe not the sad sack standing on his porch waiting for her.**

"I am very physically active and stay in excellent shape. Whether at the gym, cycling, running or doing my passion, climbing mountains, I like to maintain a high level of fitness. I have never been nor ever will be a couch potato. Since I endeavor to maintain a high fitness level, I tend to like women that also feel it important to do the same. Being a 'gym rat' isn't necessary, but if your idea of staying fit is walking to your car or going to the store, I think our fitness goals might not be the same. You get extra points if you like to dance or know the correct utensils to use at dinner. One last thing, if you absolutely love to kiss, I'm not talking just liking, I'm talking LOVING to kiss, you go to the top of the class."

**We wanted to meet this Jack Lalanne wannabe simply to challenge him to an arm-wrestling contest. We have a feeling that he may have developed his "LOVE of kissing" by practicing on photos of himself.**

"Very bright, artistic, retired professional who absolutely loves flight attendants."

**How could Bonnie pass this one up? She bought herself a stylish suit to wear on their date. When she met him for dinner in Beverly Hills, his first question was, "Oh, are you wearing your flight attendant uniform?" During the meal he was demanding and rude to the waiter, while informing her he was one of the richest men in New York City, had appeared in *Who's Who in America*, blah,blah,blah. At the end of the meal, Bonnie congratulated him on being the richest and most fabulous person in the world and hailed herself a cab.**

"I would like to have a first date with you to see if we would like to have a second. I am looking for a physical connection with a woman with dark hair, a balanced figure, fishnets and dresses to flatter her figure. I had a therapy session with a woman I was involved with and after that session of opening up and communicating, I had very intense and loving feelings. I would love you to respond. I have a lot to offer. I am handsome, active, fit and emotionally and financially secure. If not interested, I would love feedback as to why. Some women respond and some do not. I would like to know why not."

**Good question...perhaps you should ask your fishnet-wearing therapist.**

"Your letters have turned a guy who was once listed in, not one, but two "Who's Who (Real Estate and Wall Street) into a Bonnie junkie and insomniac. Well, for better or worse, I spent almost the entire night with you (well, in my mind anyway)."

**I believe he topped the list in 2005 for "Who's Who in His Own Mind."**

"Refined gentleman looking for an equal partner."

**He was waiting for me in front of an exclusive Italian restaurant. I drove up and was searching for a parking spot when I heard him bellow to the attendant at the front door, "Find her car a spot!" The attendant replied that he was not a parking valet but worked in the restaurant. This "refined gentleman" responded, "Figure it out." We entered the restaurant together and were cordially greeted**

by the host who informed us that there would be a ten minute wait for our table. My date belligerently expressed his dissatisfaction. As we waited for our table, here is what I listened to, "I am worth about $10,000,000. My grandchildren call my home 'Grandpa's Disneyland' because it is 12,000 sq. ft. Actually, I think of it more as a fortress. By the way, this is a Rolex watch I am wearing. Do you know what a Rolex is? I am quite a catch! Many women have told me that I am quite a catch. Before you, I dated a celebrity singer who told me that I was quite a catch." The bartender approached us for our drink order. I ordered a glass of Cabernet. To this, my "gentleman" sarcastically interjected, "You will need to learn how to select a fine wine." It turns out he was wrong...the Cabernet I selected looked "fine" to me as it splashed onto his suit.

# Copy and Paste

At one point all of us were dating online simultaneously. We did not want to write to the same men, so we would compare notes on those men responding to each of us. It was interesting to see that not only were the same men writing to all of us, but they were also sending us the SAME letters. Apparently Prince Charming has a form letter and he's not afraid to use it!

"Someone told me recently that if I wanted to get to know them I would have to ask the questions. Therefore, if you answer these questions I promise to send you my answers to the same questions."

Sounds harmless enough? There were 77 questions ranging from, "What weight would you consider average for a woman your height?" to "Are you a procrastinator?" I decided to write him back later.

"Please answer the following questions:
>    If you could select three people to have lunch with who would they be and why?
>    How many books have you read in the last six months?
>    Do you watch television.  If so, how often?
>    Do you exercise regularly?  If so, what type of exercise?
>    Do you like to cook?
>    What are your interests?
>    Do you have any problem arranging childcare in order to travel?
>    Where have you traveled and where do you desire to travel?
>    Do you have a problem showing affection in public?"

**I filled out the application, but I'm still waiting to hear if I got the job or not.**

"I wonder if men and/or women collect names, email addresses and phone numbers on a wall chart but then never re-contact people – like the old west with notches on the belt.  By the way, I had no intention of writing anyone today, but you have really great hair and a beautiful smile."

**Interesting to note that the photo he is referring to has NO smile.  He better re-consult his wall chart.**

"First of all, as I am sure you have been told before, you have a beautiful smile, and your eyes, well they are just gorgeous!!!!!!!"

**She <u>still</u> has NO smile in the photo. I guess the "beautiful smile" thing must be in the *Men's Guide to Making Fools of Themselves Online* handbook.**

"Aside from the obvious, that being that you are so stunningly attractive, your smile tells me that your spirit is vibrant and maybe, on occasion, somewhat mischievous"

**That is a lot to learn from a nonexistent smile! The "beautiful smile" handbook must be on the bestseller list.**

"I think a person's eyes and smile say a lot about the person they truly are. You have both of them, bright eyes and a great smile."

**I think this guy sent this same email to Mona Lisa.**

"Having such a nice smile can be contagious."

**So that's it! The "nice smile" is CONTAGIOUS and is spreading via email.**

"I'm compelled to write…its ur eyes, ur smile, ur words… they intrigue me, draw me in…what lies behind the picture."

**I can tell you this, it is certainly NOT a smile at this point.**

"I currently rent living space from a couple that met 3 years ago online. I don't need a lot of space or expensive toys to feel good about myself or my accomplishments. I'd rather be crushed by the truth than led astray by a lie. Thank you for taking the time the know more about me."

**When he says thank you for "taking the time," he is <u>not</u> kidding. His form letter email was SIX, painstaking pages long. The above excerpt was on page six. He should have just mentioned the part about renting living space in the first sentence and he could have saved us both a lot of time.**

# Your Nose is Growing

According to the majority of men we corresponded with online, they were the most fabulous group of gorgeous, wealthy, overachievers that existed on the planet. At first glance, we couldn't believe that no women had snapped these men up. Then we met them. Rather than being world-class men, they were world-class LIARS. Most men were completely unrecognizable from their descriptions of themselves. In fact, we are not even 100% sure that all of them were MEN!

"I am a 5'8", nonsmoker, good-looking professional. I live in Newport Beach, own my own company, and have a desire to live a happy, healthy life."

We talked by phone and decided to meet. When he arrived, I was sure that he was the Mayor of Munchkin City from the *Wizard of Oz*. He may be 5'8" tall standing on the hood of his car, but in person, he was shorter than my 5'2". During dinner I discovered that he lived in Newport Beach alright... in a studio above his parent's garage. He then charmed me by telling me that he had to buy his clothes and shoes in the children's department. He excused himself several times and returned smelling like smoke. He stated, "I am trying to stop, but since this would prevent me from getting dates, I put 'nonsmoker.' Just what 'Darby O'Gill and the Little People' needed, another strike against him. Needless to say, this date went up in smoke.

"Tall, handsome, educated professional...a few pounds overweight."

When we were chatting on the phone, he mentioned that he was on a diet so we decided to meet for Chinese cuisine. When I saw him, I couldn't believe that his "few pounds overweight" would have been for a man 27 feet tall. He was more like 50 pounds overweight. During dinner he ordered three different courses of food and proceeded to shovel it into his mouth. He couldn't get it in fast enough. I was afraid to stick my fork in for fear of losing a hand. He talked while chewing his food, which resulted in him spitting food at me. While I was hungry when I arrived at the date, I soon found out that the only food I would actually be able to get a bite of was the remnants of what he was spewing at me. At the end of HIS meal, my fortune cookie read, "Confucius say...you better eat this quick before your date tackles you for it!"

"Haven't you figured out that most of the men on this thing will write down anything that makes them look good? I can offer a limited warranty that all info is correct and pictures are current. I'm willing to provide Mom's phone number for verification."

**Don't think I <u>won't</u> call your mother.**

"I'm an accomplished, adorable, affluent, confident, cultured, ex-New Yorker, very young looking and in fine shape for a guy in his late 50's. I'm seeking a last great romance with an HONESTLY slim woman. Since I seem to be one of the very few in cyberspace who tell the truth, I'm 5'7", trim, very cultured and more than willing to send you a few photos of my adorable face. By the way, I also 'give great phone' so if you would like to chat, give me a call."

**Do you think that Mr. Wonderful knows what the phrase "Little Man's Complex" means?**

"I'm 5'9", toned body, blond hair."

**What attracted me to him online were his striking blue eyes. After a few phone conversations, we met for lunch. What he failed to mention was that he was 5'9" when standing on four phone books. His bright blue eyes were no longer bright blue (must have forgot the contacts) and what was left of his blond hair was gray. His "toned" body was actually a very large beer gut hanging over his belt. He**

commented on his ability to sing and mentioned having his own karaoke equipment set up in his living room.  As if that wasn't scary enough, he started belting out a few showtunes at the table.  Where was Simon Cowell when you needed him?

"Want to meet for karaoke?"

I learned through our email conversations that he loved to sing.  As a matter of fact he was another one that had his living room set up with karaoke equipment. He spoke of his parties and how everyone loved to hear him sing.  Although he was not a professional singer, he felt that he was qualified to be one.  I was excited when I agreed to meet him at a karaoke bar to hear his remarkable voice.  Once I arrived, he almost broke his neck getting up to the microphone to sing me a song.  HOLY MOTHER OF PEARL!  It was like a Kermit the Frog and Miss Piggy duet all wrapped into one voice.  Once he finished, he came back to the table beaming.  I didn't have the heart to tell him the truth, so I chose to sing a song myself to let him know my feelings... *On the Road Again*!

"Retired gentleman, handsome, salt and pepper hair looking for some good conversation."

His photos showed a very handsome man.  We agreed to meet for dinner.  I was waiting in the restaurant and through the door appeared a man with white hair.  I thought, "This couldn't be the same man that I saw in the photo." He appeared MUCH older and reminded me of my grandpa. Since his "salt and pepper" hair was completely white, I handed him the pepper shaker and told him he might want to add a little for his next date.

"My dear, you are beautiful. I could not just pass your profile without complimenting you on your beauty. I realize that I am a couple of years younger than what you are searching for, and there is also some distance between us, but if you lived here in Austin, I would be standing at your front door with a dozen, red roses. You have the warmest smile that I would imagine could light up any room or someone's life. You are one of the prettiest creations under God's celestial stars."

This young man speaks the truth. Too bad he is not old enough to vote.

"Italian stallion, looking for a meaningful relationship with one special lady."

When I met this man, I thought he was very nice. He was working out of town, but called day after day. We had a very good time when we went out together. In the midst of this, I found out that he was currently writing to one of my sisters also. He would explain that his friends were using his account and writing to other people under his name. To check out his "story", I invited him over for dinner where I displayed the very picture of my sister that he had written to. He arrived and was greeted at the door by my sister. I could see him panicking when he noticed the picture of her that he had responded to. The first words he mumbled were that his friends use his account. Riddle me this Batman, if his friends had used his account to write to my sister, how would HE recognize the photo of the girl that he DID NOT write to? Straight to the glue factory for you stallion. Ciao.

# Comedians

Who would have thought that there was so much undiscovered, comedic talent dating online? We found the following responders to be either the funniest or those who thought they were the funniest. Either way, we found ourselves laughing, either *with* them or *at* them.

"I'm new to this and just posted a profile. I'm not sure I'm going to post a photo because I'm in the Witness Protection Program. I'm 51 (that's 284 in dog years), 5'8" (5'11" in heels), athletic build, dark hair (it's all mine), Italian (no, I'm not in the Mob), brown eyes and very nice looking. At least that is what the guy in the mirror looks like. I also have all my teeth and I put the toilet seat down. Just so you know, I'm not a wacko, psycho, stalker or a car salesman."

**Points are not exactly racking up for him since my father was a car salesman. Not to mention, his email was signed, Jimmy, "The Weasel."**

"Well it all started at birth. I was born without a brain missing arms, legs and a torso, but everything else is in fantastic working order. Thanks to those red-light sales at K-mart, I have been able to shop and get replacement parts at a very good discount. When people meet me they are surprised at how well my K-mart brain functions…almost as good as a Pentium 4."

**I'm afraid, Einstein, you get what you pay for.**

"Hi there pretty lady. I think our profiles might match color if we rub them together. Of course, I need my seeing eye dog to verify this. His paw touched your profile and his body shook like you were his master. I hope we rocked your sphere."

**It will take more than a blind man and his epileptic dog to rock my world.**

"I hate to talk about myself, but since I must, here goes. I'm funny, adventurous, clean, loving, don't do drugs, don't get drunk, love conversation, go crazy for intelligent women and a great cook. In fact, the perfect mate, except for I'm moody, self-centered and superficial."

**We sound like the perfect match…especially the last part."**

"I find that this whole Internet thing starts to become a continual QVC Home Shopping Network. It becomes part of your lifestyle. The only thing we are missing is a time clock down in the right hand corner to let us know how much time is left to make a buy. There's only one of me remaining, do you want it?"

**No thanks, just browsing.**

"You are an extremely attractive lady. Had I flown with you I am sure I would have been asking you for extra peanuts, pillows, a blanket and, of course, to hold my hand on take-off and landing. Since I have never asked a flight attendant for her phone number, I guess it's best that we met in cyberspace rather than in outer space."

**At least in outerspace I could have thrown you out of the emergency exit.**

"My dog asked me to send this along. It seems he is intrigued by the photo of your pet. I have warned him of the difficulties of long-distance relationships, but he correctly reminds me that we are in Vegas frequently to visit friends. Both Harry and I will be in town over New Years. If you are at all curious about an intelligent, handsome, humorous and humble guy, let's talk."

**I would love to meet you Harry. If you insist, you can bring along your dad.**

"To your list of favorite things, I would add a woman in heels, but not when biking, swimming or gardening. I am a few inches shorter than you requested, but, honest, I will find that body stretcher someplace around here. I know I bought one because I paid the damn Visa bill for it."

**Perhaps he could borrow the heels that he wants his women to wear. Height problem solved.**

"I came across your profile and I liked it very much, along with your pictures. In looking at the pictures, I first thought your friend was a fox. Then I realized that the picture showed two good friends: one was a dog and not a fox; the other was a fox and not a dog."

**Very clever email (the photo showed Ellen with a Shiba Inu). Definitely worth a date with either the dog or the fox.**

"I'm fat, I live with my parents, am unemployed and my profile reads like *Curious George Goes Dating*, but my court-appointed therapist says I'm a real catch for some lucky woman willing to support me. Stunning is the only word to describe your picture. My pictures, on the other hand, let's just say, it takes a confident man to take such bad photos."

**I think this may be my ex-husband.**

"Well, I'm still putting in my bid to just meet you. If I get rejected, I'll either stick my tongue out at you or not change your flat tire if I see you stuck on the road."

**I have AAA, smart guy! Nah nah nah nah nah nah!**

"Your photo was an attraction, even though it appears as though you have captured a fox in the picture. I feel that any woman who likes Disney, is in the medical field and lives in Las Vegas with a 5,000 mile limit for relationships just can't be all bad! Let me know if you would like to chat, and let that poor fox go!"

**This must be the President of PETA.**

"I don't know what it is about you that makes my heart pound like a teenage boy after his first kiss. Indeed I need to know your secret. Oh my God, if my old-fashioned Greek mother was still alive, she would not believe that I said that, and, honestly, I don't believe it either. I am a very romantic person. Remember my great, great grandfather was Cupid and my great, great grandmother was either Cleopatra or Venus (not sure). I am a Greek/Eqyptian on a white horse, holding a glass slipper and looking for Cinderella. I hope you are the one (shoe size between 6-9, ring size between 5-8). Your other sizes are negotiable!"

**I have got the right shoe and ring size, but I am afraid that my Medusa hair in the morning will turn my Greek god to stone.**

# Can U Say "Spell Check?"

Sometimes the funniest part of our emails had nothing to do with what they said or how they said it, but rather how they spelled it. We warn you, fellow Americans, this does not speak well for our school systems or the intellect of our men. However, it is worthy of a little ridicule.

"wranglers hockey have you been? Would love to take you sometime if your not doing anything sataurday at 4:30 pm ill be the tall dark hanspme guy."

**Sataurday it is. I'll be the butiful gerl in the corner.**

"I am looking for someone who love's life, also enjoy's each day as it come's. She is into sports, not playing but there to saport me. I am looking to build a great friend ship and make more out of it as time go's by."

**He is the President of the "There Should Be More Apostrophes" Fan Club. Please saport his cause.**

"I know I have emailed you before you cant fault a guy for trying I know you are so the girl I hope to meet I know I fit what your looking for your beauty is awsome"

**Punctuation is overrated?**

"the things you write about your self are what I want like in a girl can we do dinner maybe catach a band I would much rather look in your eyes than type"

**I would much rather read your typing than look in your eyes. "Catach" you later.**

"I remembr lookn at yr profile & thnkn mayB we had sumthn here. I was ready 2 WINK u but thn I saw u had 3 children livn at home. But apparently Im wrong & u mayB u could b ntrestd n sum1 like me. Do call me so we can straitn ths out."

**Let's give him the benefit of the doubt. He may be missing 3 or 4 fingers, which would explain his typing. I would hate to see him bowl.**

"I had the pleasure and delight talking today. What a peasant and easy, friendly and compatible, it felt. Would you like to meet at Sturbuks for decaf?"

**Sturbuks is conveniently located directly across the street from Starbucks. It is a little less expensive since they don't have to pay for as many letters in the sign.**

"What are you doing have to go through this below the hips do you have a huffs like a horse I just can't see it. My dreams have involved you please email me back and let me know what I have to do."

**What you have to do is step away from the keyboard and "Just Say No" to drugs.**

"You are a beautiful lady. Is your photo current? I love petit women with big brests. Since I can't see your body, are you stacked? No what I mean? Most men lie but that is what we really desire. Makes my blood flow where it shud go. No what I mean? I am in good shape for my age, and am healthy. Healthy enough to be manly. No what I mean? I am what a real woman wants. I can give it to you. No what I mean?"

**I think this manly man's PENIS actually WROTE this letter itself. No what I mean?**

# Cyber-Sexual Offenders

Just when you thought that you didn't have to deal with construction workers howling and making kissing sounds as you walk by. You are about to meet the 21$^{st}$ century's version of these Neanderthals. Get ready to cringe.

"I am very athletic with a muscular physique. I sold my business and am living a carefree life in Southern California."

This was probably the best-looking man that I have ever dated. He wore his long hair in a ponytail and dressed as if he had stepped out of a magazine. On the four dates that followed, we met for dinner and dancing. There was a mutual attraction and our conversation flowed easily. Perhaps, a little too easily. On our last date, he came out with, "Are you into S & M?" My look of horror and disgust gave me away. He barked, "I can see by the look on your face that you are not!" So, I beat the hell out of him with my whip and left.

"I want a relationship with someone who shares much in common with me – plus, has a strong desire for a good sex life with her partner. Someone who will treat me like a prince in public and like her dream lover in private."

**I think the girl you are looking for charges by the hour.**

"Do you ever get told that you look a lot like this one model girl? I know her name but I'm not going to say it. You might take it the wrong way. I'll let you guess it. I mean it's a total compliment as far as I'm concerned. I think she's totally hot. Anyway, you look a lot like her."

**He sent along a photo of this "model" which actually turned out to be a porn star! The scariest part is that he had a photo of this porn star at his fingertips to email to me. By the way, the photo looked like it could have been my brother.**

"You are an amazing woman. Sexy, cool, diverse, bright and confident. I am very intrigued by you. Wow, such striking European features. I would cuddle every inch of you and introduce you to my warmth, affection, mind and spicy touch. Do you enjoy bubble baths for two while I feed you champagne and strawberries with my fingertips? Can I pamper you with lingerie, everlasting hot oil massages and roses?"

**It is NOT easy to get "striking European features" when you are born in Omaha, NE. He's laying it on thick, reader, get your hip waders on!**

"Any of you hotties looking to date a sexy, college student? I suppose, to not mislead you, I ought to add that I'm older than most of my professors. Still, you might be interested in what I might have up my sleeve or elsewhere."

**Don't skip any more classes, Copernicus. You still have a lot to learn.**

"Do you have any body shots? I have a lot of money. I'm in my prime and hung! I come to Vegas all the time, so send me your name and number!"

**Eeeeewwwww!**

"I am a handsome, 6'5" 60 year-old man who dresses impeccably. I reside in a penthouse overlooking the bright lights of the city."

**We met for lunch and there appeared to be a mutual attraction. While we were chatting, he mentioned that he wore a hearing aid and suggested that I speak a little louder and look directly at him. After an enjoyable lunch, I accepted his invitation for a second date. We met at a fine restaurant which overlooked the city. The evening was coming to a close when he told me that he had to ask me a question. "Was this for a third date," I wondered. My date, with a boyish grin, asked, "Do you like to talk dirty in bed and wear short skirts?" I smiled coyly and responded, "I don't date deviants." To this day, he is probably trying to find a woman who will talk dirty to him LOUD ENOUGH for him to hear it.**

"Are you comfortable with a kiss on the neck? If I could just push your hair aside and move your collar and inhale your scent, I would be most delighted."

**This makes me want to take a *Silkwood* shower just reading it.**

"I am a tall, charming, honest, caring professional. I own my own business and love to travel."

**After a few emails, I agreed to a phone call. The first sentence out of his mouth was, "Do you wear high, pointy shoes?" "Absolutely," I told him, "All the better to lodge up your %$#&!"**

"Hello sex goddess, wow what a horny-looking woman you are, what a pleasure it would be to make love to you...I am dreaming of it now. mmmmmmmmmm."

**This gem was signed, "Reverend Jesse Jackson."**

"I own a women's clothing line. Your eyes mesmerize me. I would love to show you my clothing line. Some women might not appreciate it, but I am hoping you will. I am a legitimate businessman and can offer you many of the finer things in life. My clothing line offers women the most sensuous gift they can offer men. My company designs and sells revealing lingerie. I would enjoy showing you my line."

**Speaking of lines, I draw one at men modeling lingerie for me.**

# 1-800-DIAL-A-DATE

Isn't it amazing that so many men just happen to be coming to Las Vegas and want to meet you. They do not correspond with you and are not interested in you UNTIL they are planning a trip here and just happen to be available for a date. Why do they think that every female living in Sin City is an escort here to provide them with a date, a tour guide, or their own personal bunny ranch. We suggest that all the men who are planning trips to Las Vegas, grab the phone and dial 1-800-DIAL-A-DATE.

"Don't let distance interfere, live near central park...anyway me sincere and find you very attractive. I will be there Thursday through Sunday at a conference. Any interest in lunch, drinks, dinner or coffee?"

That is quite an offer, but me busy.

"I wanted to try and touch base with you. I am going to be in Vegas Feb. 27th – March 3rd for the Nightclub and Bar Show. It is an incredible week of great parties. I would love it if you were up to joining me for some of them, if not all of them. I really hope you aren't taking this the wrong way. I am a classy, well-dressed gentleman and I thought we might hit it off and have some fun. P.S. I will treat you like a queen."

**What's to take the wrong way? You are looking for a date for a week-long party. I already feel like the Queen of Sheba.**

"I live in Southern California but I am in Vegas about three times a month. I come up on Friday and return Sunday. Sometimes I get there on Thursday. I think we have some things in common."

**What a coincidence...I live in Vegas but go to Southern California about three times a month. I go on Friday and return on Sunday. Sometimes I get there on Thursday.**

"I caught your personal as I was going through packing for an extended weekend trip to Las Vegas. I am in the military (Navy reserves) and had a private practice (surgeon) in Las Vegas for many years. Since Las Vegas is really my home, I will be establishing permanent residency again when the Navy retires me in 18 months. If there is some interest, drop me a line."

**Why does the government take all the good ones? When you have done your time, look me up.**

"I will be visiting Las Vegas for a conference next week and have Monday night free. Not looking for a one night thing. If you are interested, my meetings are over at 3:00 PM and would love to go to dinner and out for some fun.."

**I'll call you in your room at 2:59 PM. I hope you're there.**

"I will arrive in Las Vegas to attend the Summit Drag Races. I would be honored and happy if you would be my guest at the races any or all of the four days. They have a shareholder lounge that we can hang in with complimentary food and drink. You are so pretty and it would make me so happy just to be your friend."

**What a sweetie. Now that is an offer worth consideration.**

"Hi there. I will be in Las Vegas later this month for a poker tourney and would love to make a new friend…especially one as seemingly beautiful as you…how about a cup of coffee to start and see if there is any chemistry?"

**You've got to know when to hold 'em, know when to fold 'em. I fold.**

"Coming to Las Vegas and looking for a sugarbabe to spoil. I'll take you around the world in more ways than one. Money is no object."

**As soon as you arrive in town, jump in a cab and head to the nearest strip club. You may want to stop at an ATM on the way because "money is no object" is those girls' battle cry.**

1) "I will be in Vegas in Feb. and would love to get together with you…what do you think?"
2) "I will be in Vegas for a few days beginning March 6. I know nothing about the town. would love to meet you and have you show me the town."
3) "Hey gorgeous. You look fabulous! I'll be in Vegas September 11-13. Get back to me and we could have a wonderful time. I'll be thinking of you all day."
4) "How about dinner next Wednesday the 29th? I'll be in Vegas on business."
5) "I will be in Vegas 4/18 - 4/20. If you would like to talk or meet, call anytime."

**From the looks of these hundreds of similar emails, what happens in Vegas has been found out by the rest of the world and everybody wants a piece, so to speak.**

"I am in the process of purchasing a high-rise condo overlooking the Strip. Although, I reside in the Washington area, I hope to make my permanent home in Las Vegas."

**We met at an old-school Vegas restaurant for dinner. He had a bright and warm smile on his face. With elegant manners and charm, this man had every quality of a perfect gentleman. This was a date I wished wouldn't end. After six months of long-distance dating, the distance began to pose a problem that couldn't be solved. None of that matters, though, because I was able to make a lifelong friend who I wouldn't trade for the world.**

"I'm going to be in Vegas this weekend on business and I thought it would be fun to try and meet a nice, pretty girl on Saturday night to take out for a nice dinner and drinks and have some fun. I swear to God I'm not a sleazy person, but I broke up with my girlfriend so I figured that now is a good time to have some fun, especially since I'll be in Vegas."

**Sounds fun. I'll meet you on Fremont Street. I'll be hanging out in a mini skirt and platform shoes. Our "code phrase" will be, "Are you looking for a date?"**

# Are You For Real?

I met Mr. H for lunch on Christmas Eve day. He went on and on about how he was alone and had nowhere to go for Christmas (despite the fact that he was Jewish). I told him that I was going to my family's house for dinner to which he invited himself along. From the moment that we entered the gathering, Mr. H was trying to start trouble with everyone who was there. He methodically made his way around the party insulting the food, the people and their careers. Let it be said that our family does not unite for much, but we DID unite in our hatred for Mr. H. Nobody could even stand to look at him, let alone talk to him. While we were opening presents, he went to sleep in his chair. We were all thrilled since we no longer had to listen to him. Eventually, he woke up complaining of a headache (perhaps it was the family using his head as a piñata as he slept.) He got up to make a grand exit babbling about how he wasn't feeling well and would be leaving. As a unit, we completely ignored him as he walked to the front door. Once he was gone, we all let out a big, "HOORAY!" There really is a Santa Claus!

"You are cheating...shame on you...putting your daughter's picture on here."

**That's the oldest line in the book. Odd that it still works.**

"I'm not one to jump into a relationship just for the sake of needing to be in one. I must add that all of the ads that I've read seem to have conditions attached to them that no man could supply, unless he is Moses, Jesus or Bill Gates."

**Bill Gates, Moses and Jesus on equal turf? My word...he holds men with money in even higher regards than we do!**

"Would you be willing to pick me up at the airport sometime soon and you can treat me to lunch?"

**I think he misunderstood, "It would be nice to meet you." for "Airport taxi." Maybe I could carry his luggage for him, as well.**

"Spending a lot of time looking? I am not one of the frogs but since we don't recognize royalty in America, I am not a prince either."

**Bad news, my friend, you *may* be the unamusing wart on the frog.**

"Please fly to meet me and I'll buy you a cup of coffee."

**I am sorry to say that I must decline your offer for me to fly to California on one of *my* airline passes so that you can buy me a cup of coffee. How about you just send me the dollar, I'll buy a cup of coffee here and we'll save a lot of time.**

"We have never formally met, but in my dreams you have played every conceivable part as my companion and soul mate. I have spoken to you in my mind and have called out to you in full voice. We were linked before birth and will remain linked for all time."

**Ellen decided to give this guy a shot. They met for a charity event where he wandered off by himself for the majority of the day. They were invited out to dinner following the event, but since Mr. Wonderful had plans to see a movie, he pouted until she agreed to SKIP dinner and go to the movie he wanted to. He then said, "Don't worry about missing dinner, I'll buy you some M&M's." Let me assure you, the M&M's were the best part of this date.**

"Hi. Check out what I look like and some of my values. I do have just a touch of a left eye bruise and my chin is a bit swollen due to some surgery I had done. I did not want to wait to get a picture online. I do smile and when I get the feel back in my face, I will.."

**The eye bruise is actually what I found attractive.**

"Humorous, nice guy, loves dogs and own my own company."

**We decided to meet for dinner and drinks. When we met, he was nervous and odd, but I couldn't quite put my finger on it. When we ordered dinner my nightmare began. While he was eating he was moaning...not just small moans, but so loud that people were beginning to look. I had to bite my tongue to stop from laughing. He took a bite...mmmmm...he chewed...mmmmm...he swallows...mmmmm.... Perhaps he just got out of prison and this was his first meal in 20 years. I quickly finished my dinner and he tells me that I should take my leftovers home and put them in a plastic bag and freeze them for future dinners. Wow, I had no idea you could actually freeze things. He must have been loosening up, because he then told me that he was a Boy Scout and began to recite the Boy Scout Oath. I stopped him right there and asked him if we could go back to the moaning.**

"Looking to date a 28 to 51 year old woman. I'm looking for an individual who doesn't complain about life. Must like children (not looking for a mother). If you are into money (think that having a BMW makes you more important) and only see the world in black and white, won't try new things, and critical of differences in life, then you need to look for someone else."

**Sure...Women who like their men to have some money are FAR worse than men in their 50's looking to date 28-year olds.**

"Sexy, Catholic senior citizen looking for adventure. Had the same wife for 33 years and the same mistress for 30 years. I guess I'm into long relationships. Unfortunately, my mistress doesn't want to continue our relationship. Let's talk."

**Perhaps he should do his talking in the confessional.**

"To me, an ideal match isn't something you can sit down at a computer and describe. I can't say what she is like because I haven't met her yet. If I say I like or don't like something and some really special person passes me up because of it, then it is a lost opportunity."

**Well said!**

"When I get struck by lightning I usually like to know from whence it came. In this case, I am stunned by the beauty of the bolt."

**Corny, but it works!**

"It is a pleasure to hear from you.  Please send along a photo."

This attorney seemed interesting in our email conversations.  After sending a photo, he continued to ask for more and more photos.  After sending a few, I asked him why he was asking for so many photos.  He told me, "I am posting them all over my wall."

"P.S.  I don't like or respect FEMINIST women."

P.S.  Thank goodness that you will not be running across any of them in your dateless future!

"You sound terrific.  Would you like to go out for the day when I fly into town?"

I made a date with California man.  He wanted to spend the day together and then go to a Tom Jones concert in the evening.  We met in a casino and went to a champagne brunch buffet.  We proceeded to the cashier where California Man stood there arguing that he should not have to pay the full price since we were not going to drink the champagne.  I already wanted to head for the exit, but I was torn.  Tom Jones is my favorite performer, so I would try to make it through the date.  We spent a very long and tiring day walking around.  I told him that my feet were blistering, but he insisted on continuing to walk.  Finally, it was time to go to the show.  California Man talked to the other couple at the table while I just focused on the show.  When the show was over, I politely said, "Goodnight." Thank God for Tom Jones!

"You're beautiful, at least from the neck up. Don't be shy...give me a call."

**You are charming...at least from the MOUTH up.**

"Hello. This may be weird, but I am not a lesbian. I was playing around checking out the competition, and we seem to be a lot alike. So if you haven't fallen in love yet and you have time in your life for maybe another friend, email me."

**Sad isn't it? This poor lady has resorted to searching for girlfriends on a dating site.**

"Would love to meet those lips under the mistletoe in 2005. It is time to be bold and take my full measure."

**We do not even want to consider what "take my full measure" means. After all, you might be eating while you are reading.**

"Would love to meet you for a nice dinner and conversation. Interested?"

**Upon meeting in front of the restaurant, I noticed that my date drove up in a black, Mercedes convertible, which he could barely get out of. He was not only tall, but overweight. He exclaimed, "I am going to marry you and win you over." During dinner he mentioned that he had a prostate problem and had to sit down to urinate. Charming. He kept trying to**

get closer in the booth so I excused myself to the restroom where I called my girlfriend. I asked her to call me in five minutes with an emergency that I needed to leave for. Shortly after returning to the table, the welcomed phone call came. I apologized for my sudden departure and ran out the door.

"My, my my. Your intensity (which I find attractive) almost leaps from my computer screen. As does your reclusive, complex, seeking mind. Untrusting as you probably are, your first reaction may be, "bullshit."

I could not have said it better myself. That is quite a knowing computer he has. Perhaps it will also make him a sandwich when he's hungry.

"Does it make any sense to lie on this site only to be discovered later. Does anyone want a dishonest person who cheats or is abusive? I love pictures of people with sunglasses and big, floppy hats taken from a satellite."

I think those women wearing sunglasses and big, floppy hats are trying to hide from this gem who has resorted to stalking via satellite.

"Your smile brings a passionate sunset and sunrise for all to see along with the sunrise of each day so flower and roses will blossom for a lady like you to enthrall on your passion for life."

Run-on sentence from Edgar Allan "No Way."

"I added you to my favorite list of 4. I can't count past 8. I am looking for only 1. There are only 7 days in a week. I hope we can move you to #1."

**One, two...buckle my shoe. Three, four...there's the door!**

"My boy is 4 and lives with me 50% of the time. I should give you a calendar that's marked with my boy's schedule. You would have never known that he was sick last night by the way he was bouncing around this morning!"

**When I met this man, I thought that he was the nicest man I had ever known. He was kind, caring and adored his son. How could anyone be this perfect? Well, as our dating went on, the truth hit me like a projectile...literally. The lovely child, we'll call him Lucifer, had a very innovative way of getting his father's attention. If we were eating, he would begin to gag and throw up. If we were sitting on the couch watching T.V., he would begin to gag and throw up. While out to dinner one evening, Lucifer sat UNDER the table, threw mashed potatoes in my hair, screamed until his father took off his shirt and then as an encore, began to gag and throw up. The next day I sent a "Dear John" letter to the dad and a case of pea soup to Lucifer.**

"I am a Christian and I want a perfect Christian woman matured and really knows what a man means in her life, that she wants him to be hers and hers alone and she wouldn't go for nobody else dedicated to him and ready to do whatever pleases him."

**Why don't you just club her and drag her back to your cave?**

"You're going to shoot me. Time was running out and I hadn't heard back from you so just an hour ago I invited an old girlfriend to join me in Vegas. I really feel bad about this. Tomorrow I'm going to send you a $100 bill UPS 2-day air for any inconvenience I may have caused you. Feel free to call me and give me a piece of your mind if you care to."

**Send the $100 bill to your old girlfriend since she is the one that actually had to spend time with you.**

"I've been a veterinarian for 25 years and love dogs. Before we go to dinner, maybe I could meet your Labradoodle and give you a few tips on correcting the unruly behavior you told me about. See you tomorrow."

**This man came to pick me up and meet my dog who was making my life miserable by tearing up my rugs. When I opened the door he was smiling from ear to ear. That smile didn't last long, because after I invited him in, all hell broke loose. My Labradoodle came bounding over to greet my date. Just as he**

bent down to pet him, my dog, in one swift motion, jumped up and grabbed my date's "hair" off of his head.  Before I could process what was happening, my dog was jumping and tossing his new furry toy. My horror turned to amusement as I said to my date, "You see what I mean, he has a fetish for rugs."

"Hi there pretty lady.  Your brown eyes sparkle and what a smile…WOW…WOW…WOW…WOW…I would love to dance the night away with you.  Walk with me into the enchanted forest."

Lions and tigers and bears…OH MY.  Keep an eye out for the flying monkeys!

"Great cook wants to make you dinner."

After chatting via email, he asked me to dinner. A friend of his told him that this restaurant made delicious macaroni dishes.  He wondered if the macaroni and cheese would taste just like his mom's. His love for his mom's macaroni and cheese was one of his fondest childhood memories.  At first, I found this very touching.  During dinner he continued with stories about his mother.  Minutes seemed like hours. In between stories about his mother, he mentioned that due to his financial situation, he would not be able to take me out to dinner very often.  He would, however, be willing to cook for me as long as I rented a video to bring over.  Finally, the waitress brought the bill.  He said, "My, this is expensive.

Would you mind splitting the bill?" I split alright, but not the bill. Before I left I suggested he make a trip to the kitchen to wash dishes, just like his mother.

"How did you avoid having any wrinkles at your age?"

I divorced them all.

# Email Stalkers

Now all the fun comes to a screeching halt! This group of "matches" represents all of the angry, online daters. You don't actually have to DO anything to get them fired up. You can either respond to them or not...either way it doesn't please them. This is the dangerous part of the ride, reader. Take the safety off and proceed with caution.

"You all ask for HONESTY, yet when I give it I get shunned. What gives? I am a human being, who has learned to RESPECT other's space in this lifetime. All I ask is for the same in return. This is not rocket science. It is a dating service. Games don't evolve into love. Has any woman in Vegas ever heard of the word FAITH? If you don't have it, don't bother me. I am happy alone."

**What a relief...because I see a whole lot of "ALONE" in your future.**

"You're taking a break from dating, huh? Yeah right. And you'll still be here everyday, watch. I'm not stupid by a long shot. If I were, I wouldn't have had an illustrious career with the government for 25 years. I can't believe that you wouldn't at least take the time out and actually write me a response to my questions. But you elected to send me a computer-generated message instead. Unbelievable!!! What's the world coming to? Just no more respect or common courtesy anymore. I'm so sorry I bothered you in the first place."

**It doesn't sound like he knows too much about respect or common courtesy. "What's the world coming to?" It is coming to its senses by enacting stalker laws.**

"You're absolutely stunning, you're beautiful and drop-dead gorgeous. Even though you won't even acknowledge my presents, let alone my existence, I sincerely do wish you the best of luck."

**Presents? Did he say he has presents? Maybe I should give him a second look!**

"I see you're still here sweetheart, and I'm a fly on the wall with my fingers and toes crossed. I'll stick to the wall like glue until you're not around here anymore. And when that day comes, I hope it will be because you got tired of all the players and all the games and decided to alter your criteria ever so slightly and turn around and see that fly on the wall. You'll say to yourself, "Why not? He's a beautiful person.""

Then you will say, "I'm sorry I just didn't take a very good look at you before so please forgive me and let's go."

**Where did I put my fly swatter?**

"Hello. I sent you a WINK. I noticed that you viewed my profile, but have not responded. I thought we make an attractive and classy match. I would enjoy hearing something from you."

**Sounds harmless, right? Keep reading.**

"Hello. I have winked at you. I BELIEVE YOU HAVE CHECKED OUT MY PROFILE. Are you ever going to communicate?"

**The gloves are coming off.**

"Hello again. Hope you are well. Wondering if you will write back. A 'no thanks' is better than leaving a person hanging."

**It doesn't stop here.**

"HELLO AGAIN. YES, NO, MAYBE? Is it too much trouble to take two seconds to answer a nice gentleman? I want to hear something from you."

**The CAPS LOCK is getting worse.**

"HELLO. YOU ARE A TRUE DUD!! NO COMMU-NICATION SKILLS WHATSOEVER!!! People like you make on-line dating a DRAG!!! SHAME ON YOU!!!"

**The CRESCENDO is coming!**

"HELLO. UNFORTUNATELY, YOU ARE MUCH TOO SLOW WITH YOUR COMMUNICATION. It seems your intention is to NOT meet a very nice gentleman. GOOD LUCK WITH THE SCRAGGLY JERKS ON THIS WEBSITE!! YOU LOSE!!"

**Speaking of "scraggly jerks"…I am quite sure that he is poking pins into little dolls with our pictures taped to their heads!**

# Give Them the Boot!

In our online travels, we went on many dates and had numerous relationships. Along the way, we had to cut some of our suitors loose either via email or in person. We thought you might enjoy a few of those stories. In addition, we will share with you a few of the brush-offs that we received, as SHOCKING as that is.

"Recently divorced, romantic but realistic professional. My partner would be accepting of others, my friends, and my children. A positive outlook is a must."

When I met this doctor out for dinner, I was surprised that he brought along a female friend of his for our date. While odd, the date went well and I agreed to meet him again. Lo and behold, on our second date, he again showed up with this woman. She spent the evening disparaging him and trying to convince me not to date him. She mentioned that with the home she was selling him, he would be broke. Believe it or not, I accepted a third date because the man seemed very pleasant. When I arrived for our third date, little Miss Mary Sunshine was attached to his hip once again. I graciously told Dr. Double Date that while he seemed very nice, I was going to have to break it off with his woman puppet. I had always wondered what happened to "Madam" when Wayland Flowers died. Now I know.

"I could tell that there was no love connection on our date as our conversation became very one-sided on my part. I also detected a lack of interest from you. I can't help but comment that you are really quite attractive and have everything going for you, but you should consider some better pictures. You will then be able to pick and choose your next companion."

Allow me to make a suggestion as well. You may want to consider adding a photo to your profile of the posterior of a pony. By doing this, your future dates will be able to recognize you quickly.

"I haven't had a birthday party, cake or presents for years."

We dated for nearly a year during which time he had a birthday. I asked him what his favorite type of cake was and he told me his mother used to make him an applesauce cake when he was growing up. I experimented with three different recipes to get the one that tasted just right. I found him the perfect gifts and took photos of him at his birthday party. After dating for some time, my sister noticed that his photo was back online. To add insult to injury, the new photo was the one I had taken of him standing next to the cake that *I* made and the presents that *I* bought. Now I fully understand why he had not had a birthday party, cake or presents for years. That must have been the last time some woman fell for this momma boy's "applesauce cake" story. The following is the email I sent to him.

"No matter which way you twist or turn things, the outcome is obvious. For some reason, you like to stay glued to online dating. I don't know if you like the attention that it provides you, but I do know that honesty is something I cannot compromise on. Whether a friendship or a committed relationship, this has the feeling of being one-sided. I only wish good things for you."

That translates to, "I wish good riddance and hope your next "date" is a drag queen."

"I would love to fly in to meet you. I will show you what a great pair we make."

Thank you for your offer. When we spoke, you mentioned so many wonderful qualities that you possess and all of the wonderful things that your money can buy. The bad news is that I do not think we will make the perfect match. However, the good news is that you and your mirror are made for each other.

"My name is AspenBob. I am a retired former business owner. I spend time enjoying my homes in Mexico, Arizona, Florida and Aspen. I am looking to share my life with a soul mate."

**After several emails, he drove from Arizona to meet. We went to dinner and a Vegas show. We seemed to be having a great time and he had the photographer take 8X10 and wallet photos of us. He was anxiously making plans to visit again the following weekend. I never heard from him again. I did notice, however, that a week later AspenBob no longer existed on the Internet. A new profile called CaboBob had taken his place.**

"Thank you for a lovely evening. I find you attractive, sophisticated, intelligent and I enjoy your company. Although we have many common interests, my lifestyle is quite opposite of yours. You mentioned dating others and I am looking for a one-on-one relationship. I wish you the best of luck."

**Once again, the translation is, "I wish you the best of luck with your future STD."**

"I am a retired teacher, average build, 5'9". My interests include music, dancing and theater."

**We decided to meet for lunch. When he entered the restaurant, I realized that half of him was missing. Being that he was about 5'2", where did**

the other seven inches go?  Our conversation was strained and a minute seemed like an hour.  When lunch was finally over, he walked me to my car.  He ended up being parked right next to me.  When he opened his door, I noticed a phone book on the seat.  He chuckled and told me that he had to sit on it to see over the steering wheel!  How did he reach the pedals...broomstick handles?

"I don't think my profile would sway your decision to dump me which you have already obviously made.  Have a great life."

**It is already starting to look up.**

"I am the perfect, divorced man...handsome...late forties... I have a private jet and a house on the beach."

**He flew into town to meet me.  He had dinner and drinks served in his suite.  The fun didn't stop there.  We went to a fabulous show and had a nice evening.  He was a perfect gentleman and I couldn't wait to see him again.  He flew me to L.A. for our second date where a limo whisked me to his beachfront home.  Does this sound too good to be true?  It was.  He is NOT divorced, but rather remains in divorce court, where he has been for three years.**

"Southern Californian who loves jazz, playing the saxophone and riding my Harley."

We exchanged photos and emails for a few weeks when suddenly the emails stopped. A few weeks later an email arrived apologizing for being so busy and asking if I was still available. He then started to call regularly. He would play jazz songs to me saying, "This one is just for you." He made plans to visit Las Vegas and seemed anxious to meet me. That is the second that the calls and emails stopped. I saw his picture one more time...on the wall at the post office.

"Northern California attorney who is attractive and bright."

After several lengthy emails and phone conversations, he invited me to San Francisco for a baseball game. He made arrangements for two hotel rooms. Our weekend was exciting and there was great chemistry. For several months after our trip, he drove to Las Vegas on weekends and we had a lot of fun. I thought that distance was our only obstacle right up until the moment he fell off the planet never to be heard from again.

"I am a true gentleman who loves to travel. I'm looking for a lady to see the world with me."

We met and seemed to hit it off. After a few months of dating, we decided to take a weekend trip to Catalina. On the road trip to Long Beach, he brought a thermos of Bloody Mary's and green beans (to put in the Bloody Mary's). What I discovered was that all of his meals consisted of alcohol, and a little bit of food thrown in for good measure.

During our trip to Catalina, he would receive calls on his cell phone at 1:00 AM. When he hung up, he would say that it was an employee calling. Never mind that he didn't own his own company. If it weren't for the sharks, I would have swum for the coast. Oh, the hell with the sharks!.

"I am a disc jockey who loves music and dancing. I would love to dance the night away with you."

He invited me to a singles dance that he was sponsoring and spinning records at. It was a great night filled with fun and laughter. He dedicated romantic songs to me and even joined me for a few dances. At the end of the evening, we agreed to a second date. He called me a few nights later and invited me to another dance function. I was really looking forward to spending time with this charismatic man. He asked me to meet him at the dance half an hour early. When I arrived he met me at the door with great anticipation. As we walked in, he told me that he would give me half-price admission if I would work in the kitchen and serve refreshments. After all, I could spend half of the evening on the dance floor and save $5.00. So let me get this straight...$5.00 for two hours of work? His next dancing date was with the Department of Labor.

"Can I please ask what your sign is?????"

# Happy Endings

What a wild ride! The three sisters, Candace, Bonnie and Ellen, took online dating to a new level. There was laughter and tears (mostly the tears came from laughing too hard). Remember this, there are fabulous "matches" out there waiting for you to email them. You just have to mine a lot of coal to get to the diamonds.

"I started this project with a less-than-positive outlook. Despite the "mismatches" we have amused you with, I still believe that you can find true love online. Hope springs eternal!

Somewhere out there is my prince. Unfortunately, he is still trying to make his way through the 10,732,446 frogs surrounding me!"

*Candace*

"This experience has opened doors into relationships that I would have never explored. Even though some doors slammed shut, and some would have been better off remaining closed, it was a positive experience for me.

I have met Mr. Multiple Dater, Mr. Not So Perfect and Mr. Wrong. I must keep the faith, however, because I know Mr. Right is out there. Maybe his computer is broken right now. I will forge ahead in my quest. Wish me luck!"

*Bonnie*

"With very little 'free' time in my life, I thought that online dating would be perfect for me. I found myself excited to come home and check the computer for my responses. Granted, I have had some failures with my "matches," but I am still hopeful for a true happy ending.

Online dating has opened up a whole wide world for me to search for my perfect partner. After all, what are the odds that he will be in my neighborhood taking out his trash as I walk my dog? The dream is still alive!"

*Ellen*